Embracing the Power of Patience in a Fast-Paced World

WAIT

Take a Purposeful Pause

DEEPAK OJHA

ISBN
Paperback 979-8-89556-343-4
Hardcase 979-8-89632-738-7

Contents

Foreword by Dr Rajesh Kumar, IPS

ডঃ রাজেশ কুমার, আইপিএস
Dr. Rajesh Kumar, IPS

Principal Secretary
Environment Department
Government of West Bengal

Foreword

It is with great pleasure that I pen this foreword for **WAIT: Take a Purposeful Pause, authored by Shri Deepak Ojha.** I have had the privilege of knowing Deepak and his family for many years, particularly his father, Shri Sushil Ojha, a close family friend. Over the years, I have seen Deepak grow from a young man into a mature business leader, successfully balancing his responsibilities in both business and his passion for eSports.

Deepak's journey has been nothing short of inspiring. Today, he manages a successful business involved in the manufacturing of lead, a vital raw material for battery production and certain PVC products. With the rapid rise in demand for e-vehicles, Deepak's business has flourished, boasting a turnover of ₹400 crore this year, and the future looks even brighter. Despite the rigours of running this large-scale enterprise, Deepak has never lost sight of his personal interests. He also runs TalkEsport (https://www.talkesport.com), a prominent web portal dedicated to the growing world of eSports, which further demonstrates his ability to seamlessly manage both his business and his passion.

WAIT: Take a Purposeful Pause reflects Deepak's unique ability to find balance in a fast-paced world. This book isn't just about the idea of waiting; it's about purposeful, mindful pauses that can lead to growth and better decision-making. It provides valuable insights into how patience and reflection can foster not only personal growth but also professional success. Deepak's reflections are drawn from his own journey, making this book a powerful and relatable guide for anyone seeking to navigate life's complexities with greater wisdom.

In a time when the world is constantly pushing for speed and instant results, Deepak encourages us to slow down and embrace the moments of stillness that life offers. His thoughtful exploration of patience as a tool for growth resonates deeply, especially in fields where long-term vision and careful planning are essential—whether it's the environmental

PRANI SAMPAD BHAVAN, 5th Floor, LB-2, Sector III, Salt Lake, Kolkata-700 106
Ph.: (033) 2335 2742, Fax : (033) 2335 0271   E-mail : Psecy.env-wb@gov.in

ডঃ রাজেশ কুমার, আইপিএস
Dr. Rajesh Kumar, IPS

Principal Secretary
Environment Department
Government of West Bengal

challenges I face in my work, or the strategic decisions required in business.

I have had the privilege of witnessing Deepak's evolution, and his personal and professional accomplishments speak volumes about his determination, vision, and ability to adapt in a world of constant change. His success in managing both a thriving business and a web portal dedicated to eSports is a testament to his dynamic and multifaceted personality.

This book will undoubtedly offer readers practical strategies to approach life with greater calm, purpose, and clarity. I highly recommend **WAIT: Take a Purposeful Pause** to anyone looking to cultivate the art of waiting and make more deliberate, impactful decisions in both their personal and professional lives.

Dr. Rajesh Kumar, IPS
Principal Secretary,
Department of Environment,
Govt. of West Bengal

PRANI SAMPAD BHAVAN, 5th Floor, LB-2, Sector III, Salt Lake, Kolkata-700 106
Ph.: (033) 2335 2742, Fax : (033) 2335 0271   E-mail : Psecy.env-wb@gov.in

Preface

Patience is often described as a virtue, a skill to be cultivated, a practice to be mastered. But patience, as I have come to understand it, is much more than that. It is an active engagement with life itself—a willingness to embrace uncertainty, navigate the unknown, and trust in something larger than ourselves. In a world that glorifies speed, quick decisions, and immediate results, the idea of waiting can feel almost radical. Yet, it is in these very moments of pause that life often reveals its most profound lessons.

When I began this journey of writing *WAIT*, I realised that patience had been the silent teacher in all my experiences. From humble beginnings, with my first paycheck of just INR 3,500, to navigating the complexities of capital markets, media, and manufacturing, I have been guided by a simple yet powerful idea: that waiting is not about doing nothing; it is about doing everything with a sense of purpose and timing. It's about knowing that growth often happens in the pauses, in the spaces where we are not rushing but observing, learning, and allowing things to unfold.

This book is not about me, though it is rooted in my experiences. It is about the universal journey we all undertake—the journey of living, learning, and discovering who we are meant to be. It is about understanding that we are part of a much larger story, a cosmic dance that moves in rhythms and cycles far beyond our immediate comprehension. My fascination with astronomy, the stars, and Carl Sagan's *Pale Blue Dot* has given me a perspective that we are but a speck in the vast expanse of the universe. And yet, within that smallness, there is something infinitely meaningful.

WAIT is not a definitive guide, nor does it offer a one-size-fits-all approach to life. Instead, it is a collection of reflections, practical lessons, and stories from my journey—an exploration of how patience has shaped my path and how it can shape yours, too. It is an invitation to see waiting not as a hindrance but as an opportunity to engage more deeply with life, to trust in the timing of the universe, and to find peace in the moments of stillness.

My hope is that this book will offer you a new lens through which to view your own pauses and waiting periods. Whether you are at a crossroads, in a transition, or simply feeling stuck, remember that every pause has its purpose, and every moment of stillness holds the potential for growth. - Deepak Ojha

About the Author

Deepak Ojha is an entrepreneur, philanthropist, author, and passionate explorer of life's many facets. From humble beginnings, he embarked on a diverse professional journey that spanned capital markets, garment and medicine retail, website design, marketing, social media, writing, and journalism. This eclectic path led him to his current role in manufacturing, where he serves as a key figure in steering the growth and transformation of an established company.

Deepak is driven by a deep curiosity and a relentless pursuit of growth, both personal and professional. He embraces life with a philosophical outlook, drawing inspiration from his love for cricket, philanthropy, and his vivid fascination with cosmology and the mysteries of the universe. As a firm believer in the power of patience and reflection, he sees each experience as an opportunity for growth, whether it involves running a business, writing a book, or navigating life's unpredictable turns.

With his debut book, *WAIT*, Deepak adds another dimension to his journey, sharing his insights on the art of patience and the wisdom of waiting. He approaches his roles—both in business and as an author—with a profound belief in a greater force at work, trusting the universe's timing and finding meaning in every moment.

Special Mention

Shri Rajendra Khandelwal
Your inspiring personality has left an indelible mark on me; thank you for being a beacon of positivity.

Prelude: The Path to Patience

In the dense, mist-laden forests of China, there is a remarkable tree, the Chinese bamboo. Its story is a profound lesson in patience, persistence, and the unseen work that takes place beneath the surface. For five years after the seed is planted, nothing seems to happen. No matter how diligently it is watered, fertilised, and tended, the bamboo shows no visible signs of growth. Day after day, the caretaker must trust that something is happening, even if they cannot see it.

During these five years, it would be easy to give up and think that all the effort and nurturing have been in vain. And yet, this is precisely the period when the bamboo is laying its foundation. Below the surface, the roots are growing deep, spreading wide, fortifying themselves to support the growth that is to come. And then, after five long years, something miraculous happens. Almost overnight, the bamboo shoots up, growing over 80 feet tall in just six weeks.

Did it grow 80 feet in six weeks? Or did it take five years and six weeks? The truth is it took every day of those five years for the bamboo to establish the strength it needed to soar. Without the invisible work happening beneath the surface, the sudden visible growth would never be possible.

This story of the bamboo tree is not merely about waiting. It is about waiting with intention, with faith, and with a clear plan. The bamboo does not grow in isolation; it is nurtured continuously, cared for every day, even when there are no visible results. The lesson here is profound: patience alone is not enough. It is the patience combined with purposeful action that ultimately leads to growth.

Much like the bamboo, we too have our seasons of quiet growth, times when it feels as if nothing is happening despite our best efforts. But these are the moments when our roots are deepening, when we are preparing for the growth that is to come. The journey requires not just waiting, but being patient with the right mindset, knowing that every step, every moment, and every effort counts—even when the results are not immediately visible.

In the chapters that follow, I invite you to explore this idea of waiting with purpose. Waiting is not about passivity; it's about trusting the process, nurturing your dreams, and preparing for the moment when life will allow you to rise. Like the bamboo tree, your growth may not always be visible to the world, but know that every day of patient effort is building the foundation for something extraordinary.

How To Navigate This Book

WAIT is not just a book to be read; it's a journey to be lived. My hope is that, as you move through each chapter, you don't just find yourself skimming through words, but truly engaging with your own thoughts, feelings, and experiences of what it means to wait.

Each chapter is a piece of a larger puzzle—crafted from stories of my journey, lessons learned, and reflections drawn from the experiences of others. These are not tales merely meant to be told but experiences to be felt, lessons to be reflected upon, and ideas to be tested in the crucible of your own life.

After each chapter, you will find a few elements that are there to help you dive deeper and engage with the content more personally. I've added reflection prompts to guide you through thinking about your own experiences with patience. Think of these as gentle nudges, questions that might make you pause, reflect, or even smile. There's no rush to answer them, no right or wrong way—just an invitation to explore your own thoughts. You might find it helpful to write them down, discuss them with a friend, or simply sit quietly and let them wander through your mind.

Then come the exercises. These are not meant to burden you but to give you a real sense of how patience might feel in practice in those small, everyday moments. Think of them as little experiments—try them out in your daily life and see what happens. Maybe you'll discover something new about yourself, or maybe you'll just enjoy the process.

I've also included a few frequently asked questions at the end of each chapter—questions I've encountered over the years, the kinds of things people often wonder about when we talk about patience. These are here to help you think through some of the doubts or curiosities that might come up for you, to offer some clarity, or perhaps to spark a new question altogether.

And lastly, you will find a closing story or anecdote – a small tale from history or a lesson from someone who has walked a similar path. These are here to remind you that patience is a shared human experience, one that connects us all across time and place. They're here to inspire you, to show you that waiting has shaped lives, decisions, and outcomes in countless ways.

And, just as each chapter begins with an open door, it ends with a Closing Thought – a moment to gather what we've explored, to see where we've been, and to ponder where we might be going next. Think of these as small reminders that this journey is not about finding all the answers but about embracing the questions, the pauses, and the moments in between.

This book is meant to be taken slowly. There is no rush. Move through the chapters at your own pace. Take your time with each reflection, each exercise, each story. Let yourself linger where you feel called to linger. This is not a race but a gentle unfolding, a journey toward understanding, a practice of patience itself.

As you read, remember that each page is an invitation—to pause, to reflect, to wait. Find your own rhythm and flow, and trust that in this waiting, there is wisdom, growth, and a deeper connection to life's unfolding.

In the end, patience is not just about waiting; it's about living fully in the moments that waiting brings to us.

CHAPTER 1

Introduction – The Power of Patience

Patience is often seen as a passive virtue, a quiet endurance in the face of adversity. But I've learned over the years that patience is much more dynamic – it's a strategic pause, a thoughtful delay that can change the course of events. It is about choosing to wait, not because we are unsure or afraid, but because we are wise enough to understand the power of the pause.

I recall the early days of my career, fresh out of high school and eager to prove myself. I thought confidence meant being quick with my words and immediate with my reactions. During meetings, I would jump in at the first opportunity, trying to make my mark. In conference rooms filled with seasoned professionals, my instinct was to be the first to respond, to show that I was sharp, that I was present.

But looking back, I realise that many of those early reactions were born out of insecurity rather than insight. In my haste to speak, I often missed the subtler currents in the room—the unspoken concerns, the hidden agendas, the silent negotiations that happen behind every exchange. Each time I jumped in too quickly, I found myself caught off guard, often regretting my words or actions later. The repercussions were not just immediate; they echoed through my professional relationships, sometimes causing damage that took years to repair.

A Costly Lesson in Impatience

One incident stands out vividly in my memory. I was in a high-stakes negotiation meeting with a potential client, a deal that could have opened new avenues for my company. I was well-prepared and confident. As the meeting began, the client raised several points that challenged our proposal. I could feel my heart rate quicken, the rush of adrenaline urging me to defend our position. Without thinking, I interrupted the client, eager to counter their objections with facts and figures.

What followed was a painful silence, one that stretched out longer than I expected. The client, visibly displeased, cut the meeting short. Later, I learned that my haste had been perceived as arrogance. They felt I had not taken the time to truly understand their concerns or demonstrate respect for their perspective. That deal, which could have been a turning point, slipped through my fingers. It took me a long time to realise that my rapid response had betrayed a lack of patience, a lack of wisdom.

Over time, I began to notice a pattern. In meetings where I chose to wait—to listen fully, to absorb not just the words but the intentions behind them—I found myself more prepared, more centred. The more I waited, the clearer I became about what needed to be said, and, more importantly, what didn't need to be said.

Another Instance: Letting Ideas Breathe

There was another instance in a board meeting that I remember vividly. One of the co-directors, who also happened to be a minor shareholder, proposed the idea of converting part of our factory land into a cold storage warehouse. I responded immediately. I had already considered this option and knew it wasn't viable; the traffic congestion in the surrounding area made it impractical for such a facility.

In my haste to prove that I had thought of this before, I quickly pointed out the potential traffic problems, aiming to shut down the idea immediately. While my observation was accurate and pragmatic, the feedback I received later was that my response seemed abrupt and dismissive. I was told that my reaction had come across as negative and had stifled a colleague's initiative.

One of my peers offered a piece of advice that stuck with me. He suggested that instead of outright rejecting the proposal, I could have let the idea develop. By allowing my colleague to explore the feasibility of the project, I could have fostered a sense of contribution and collaboration. "Sometimes," he said, "people just want to see their ideas considered, even if they eventually die out on their own. It's less about the outcome and more about the process."

That moment taught me a valuable lesson. While I was correct in my assessment, the narrative that emerged was one of impatience and negativity. I realised that patience is not just about what you say, but how and when you say it. By waiting, by allowing ideas to breathe—even if they are ultimately unworkable—we create an environment where people feel heard and valued.

The Reward of Waiting: A Million-Dollar Win

Patience doesn't just prevent mistakes; sometimes, it leads to unexpected rewards. There was a memorable occasion when our patience in a negotiation paid off in a way I could never have anticipated. We were in discussions with a major overseas client over a substantial order. Our market intelligence suggested a pricing strategy that was considerably lower than what we hoped for. The temptation to quickly accept the price they hinted at was strong; it was still a significant order, and we didn't want to risk losing it.

However, something told me to wait. Instead of rushing to agree, I chose to listen closely, to gauge their tone, and to let the silence do some of the talking. I asked a few questions and let the conversation flow without showing our hands too soon. As the meeting progressed, the client, perhaps sensing our hesitation, unexpectedly revealed that they had budgeted significantly higher for this project than our intelligence had suggested.

That pause, that strategic patience, saved us from under-pricing our product. By waiting and allowing the client to lead the conversation, we ended up securing the order at a much higher price than we initially anticipated—resulting in millions of additional revenue. Had we jumped at the first opportunity, eager to close the deal, we would have left a substantial amount on the table.

This experience taught me that patience in negotiations isn't just about delaying decisions; it's about creating a space where the best outcome can emerge naturally. It showed me that sometimes, the best strategy is simply to wait – to let the other side reveal their cards, to allow the situation to develop before making a move.

Learning from a Friend: The Power of Silence in Personal Life

Much of my understanding of patience in personal interactions has come from observing and learning from close relationships. I've noticed that some of the most meaningful conversations happen when we allow space for silence, giving the other person time to express themselves fully. It's interesting how the longer we speak without interruption, the more we tend to lose clarity and purpose in our words. Often, we reach a point where we are merely filling the silence rather than adding real value to the conversation.

This realisation taught me the profound gift of waiting and truly listening. By allowing others to speak without interruption, we give them a sense of completeness, of being fully heard. This simple act of patience creates an environment where people feel secure and valued, and it opens the door for deeper, more meaningful connections.

I've also observed the opposite in my early career, where I noticed colleagues who were quick to interrupt, eager to contribute, or to argue, often believing that their input would always add value to the discussion. But over time, I learned that speaking our minds doesn't always mean speaking with sense. Often, it just means we're letting out whatever is inside us, whether it's relevant or not. By giving someone the time and space to speak, we offer them something far more valuable – a feeling of security and the understanding that their thoughts truly matter.

This lesson in patience has significantly shaped my approach to communication. By choosing to wait, to listen more, and to speak less, I found that people opened up more, relationships deepened, and trust grew stronger. The more I practised this, the more meaningful our conversations became. Patience, in this sense, is a silent power—a quiet force that fosters understanding and connection.

The Preparedness of Waiting

The more I've practised patience, the more I've come to realise that waiting doesn't make us weaker; it makes us stronger. In negotiations, interviews, or any situation where stakes are high, the ability to wait—to truly listen before we speak—becomes a source of immense power. The longer I wait, the more prepared I feel, and the more aligned my words become with my intentions.

Patience is not about holding back; it's about holding steady. It's about knowing that sometimes the best response is no response at all, at least not immediately. It's about allowing the situation to unfold, to reveal its true nature before we decide how to act.

In a world that often values speed over substance, patience is a radical choice. But it is a choice that pays dividends. The next time you feel the urge to react, to respond, to jump in—wait. Wait just a moment longer. You may find that what you were about to say is not what you truly needed to say. And in that wait, you may discover a wisdom you never knew you had.

Reflection Prompts:

1. Reflect on a time when waiting brought unexpected results. What did you learn from that experience?
2. How do you currently perceive patience in your daily life? Is it a struggle, a strength, or something in between?

Exercise:

▷ **Daily Patience Practice:** Over the next week, identify moments when you feel impatient. Note what triggers these feelings and practice breathing deeply, counting to five before reacting. Record your thoughts at the end of each day about any changes you notice.

FAQ:

Q: Why is patience considered a strength and not a weakness?
A: Patience is a strength because it involves self-control, emotional intelligence, and a deep understanding of timing. It allows you to choose your responses rather than reacting impulsively, often leading to better decisions and healthier relationships.

Mandela's Approach

Nelson Mandela, South Africa's first black president and a Nobel Peace Prize winner, is often celebrated for his patience, which he demonstrated throughout his 27 years in prison. Arrested in 1962 for his anti-apartheid activities, Mandela faced a life sentence at Robben Island, a notorious prison where he endured harsh conditions, hard labour, and isolation from his family and supporters.

Despite the unjust incarceration, Mandela chose a path of patience. He realised that responding with anger or hatred would only fuel further division and conflict. Instead, he used his time in prison to study, reflect, and develop a deep understanding of his political adversaries. He learned their language (Afrikaans) to better communicate with them, read extensively, and engaged in discussions with his fellow prisoners. He also maintained a sense of dignity and calmness that earned him the respect of both his fellow prisoners and even some of the guards.

Mandela's patience was not passive – it was a strategic choice. He understood that the fight against apartheid was a long game, and waiting with purpose would serve his cause better than immediate reaction or violence. Upon his release in 1990, after years of negotiations, Mandela chose a path of reconciliation rather than retribution, a decision that ultimately paved the way for a peaceful transition to democracy in South Africa.

Mandela's patience not only helped dismantle apartheid but also prevented a Civil War, leaving a legacy of forgiveness, dialogue and perseverance. His story exemplifies how patience, even in the most challenging circumstances, can lead to monumental change.

Closing Thoughts

Patience is not just about enduring the wait; it's about strategically using that time to learn, grow, and prepare for what comes next. Whether in the boardroom or in personal relationships, patience allows us to see beyond immediate impulses and make decisions rooted in wisdom.

As we move through this book, remember that every pause is an opportunity for growth, and every wait is a chance to strengthen your understanding. Patience is your most powerful ally. Let's explore how to harness it fully.

CHAPTER 2

Wait Before You React: Preserving Relationships

There is a saying that the first thought that comes to mind is often not the wisest. Over time, I have come to realise that the immediate urge to react – to speak out, defend, or argue – is seldom the best course of action, especially when it comes to the relationships that matter most. Whether it's with a spouse, friends, parents, or siblings, waiting before reacting has proven, time and again, to be a powerful practice in maintaining and strengthening these bonds.

The Wisdom of Patience in Relationships

In the *Bhagavad Gita*, Lord Krishna advises Arjuna, "One who is not disturbed by happiness and distress and is steady in both is certainly eligible for liberation." While the context here is spiritual, it resonates deeply with the day-to-day dynamics of relationships. Life constantly presents us with situations that provoke emotional reactions. But true wisdom, as Krishna implies, lies in maintaining steadiness—choosing not to be swayed by the immediate impulse to react.

I have seen in my life how reacting hastily, especially in moments of anger, frustration, or anxiety, often leads to regret. A reaction fuelled by emotion can cause unintended harm, create misunderstandings, and even fracture the foundation of trust that relationships are built upon.

Waiting with Friends: The Power of Silence Amidst Misunderstanding

One of the most challenging aspects of friendships can be navigating misunderstandings, especially when they are compounded by gossip or sceptical comments. I learned a profound lesson about the power of silence from a situation with a group of close friends. A misunderstanding fuelled by miscommunication and a few misguided comments.

Initially, I felt the strong urge to defend myself, to clear the air, and to confront those who had spread the gossip. I wanted to set things right immediately, to make sure everyone knew my side of the story. But something held me back. I remembered the lessons life had taught me: that silence often carries a power of its own, and that not all battles need to be fought with words.

Instead of reacting, I chose to remain silent—not in a way that shut down communication, but in a way that did not add fuel to the fire. I continued to engage with my friends as I normally would, but I refrained from addressing the gossip directly. I was careful not to retaliate or speak ill of anyone despite the temptation. I wanted my actions to reflect my true intentions, believing that over time, the truth would reveal itself.

And it did. Slowly, the misunderstandings began to unravel on their own. Friends who had been sceptical began to realise that the rumours lacked substance. As days passed, the tension eased, and the situation gradually diffused without any direct confrontation. By choosing silence and patience, I allowed the truth to emerge naturally. The power of waiting, of not reacting in the face of unjust treatment, preserved our friendships and prevented unnecessary conflict.

Had I reacted immediately, the chances were high that the situation could have escalated, possibly leading to irreparable damage to our relationship. Instead, my silence communicated that something was amiss—that things were not right and needed to be addressed—but it did so without accusation or defensiveness. It allowed room for reflection and understanding to grow in its own time.

I learned that silence doesn't mean the absence of communication; it can be a form of communication itself. It conveys strength, restraint, and confidence in the truth. It shows that one does not need to react to every provocation or engage with every piece of gossip. In this silence, there is immense power—a power that can mend relationships, bridge gaps, and foster deeper connections.

Family Matters: The Practice of Waiting with My Father

A few years ago, my father suggested a radical approach to a problem I had encountered. I was at a critical juncture, deciding whether to pursue a new business venture or stay on my current path. My father, with his wisdom and experience, offered his perspective during one of our conversations.

He proposed a course of action that seemed completely out of sync with my own ideas. His suggestion felt outdated, even risky, from my point of view. My first instinct, shaped by years of headstrong decision-making, was to dismiss his advice outright. In the past, I might have reacted hastily, letting my words come out harsh and defensive, keen to protect my own approach.

But something in me had changed. I had begun to understand the power of waiting before reacting, especially with those closest to me. Instead of jumping to conclusions or arguing, I decided to listen. I allowed my father to express his full thoughts, refraining from interrupting or defending my stance. I watched his expressions and took in the careful way he laid out his reasoning.

As I listened with patience, something shifted within me. I began to see that his advice wasn't as radical as I had initially thought. His approach was grounded in logic, built upon years of experience that I had perhaps taken for granted. He was advocating for a solution that, while different from my own, had a rationale worth considering. He wasn't just throwing out suggestions; he was drawing from his understanding of the market, the competition, and the broader picture that I was too close to see.

Had I reacted immediately, I would have missed the wisdom in his words. I realised that his suggestion wasn't about questioning my abilities or undermining my confidence. It was about offering me a perspective that came from a place of deep care and concern—a different lens through which to view my situation. My patience allowed me to absorb his ideas, think them through, and weigh their merit.

By waiting to respond, I found myself not in opposition to his ideas but in dialogue with them. We were able to discuss his suggestions openly, examining the pros and cons together. This time, instead of a heated debate, we had a meaningful conversation. His advice ultimately influenced my decision, blending with my own approach to create a more robust plan than I had initially imagined.

At that moment, I realised that my father's counsel had always been rooted in love and rationality, even if it did not always align with my perspective. My patience allowed me to see the rationality in what once seemed radical, to approach his advice with an open mind, and to respond in a way that strengthened our bond rather than strained it.

Siblings: Understanding Through Patience

When we think about the concept of waiting, it's easy to overlook the subtle, everyday ways it plays out within our relationships with siblings. Growing up with siblings, we often learn the value of waiting in ways we don't even realise. From sharing a single piece of cake to waiting for our turn to speak during heated family discussions, these interactions lay the groundwork for understanding patience as a powerful force.

In many ways, the patience learned from these simple acts of waiting is preparation for the complexities of adult relationships. For instance, siblings often find themselves in different cities, working in different professions, or living different lifestyles. These differences can lead to misunderstandings or feelings of disconnection. Yet, the patience they learned growing up—the ability to wait, to listen, to let things settle before reacting—helps them maintain a strong bond despite the distance or changes in their lives.

Waiting becomes essential when life changes occur—like one sibling facing a challenging career decision, another experiencing a major personal transition, or even when both are raising their own families in a world that moves at a relentless pace. In these times, the ability to wait, to give each other the time and space to figure things out, becomes crucial. It's not about waiting in silence or avoiding difficult conversations; it's about trusting that, with time, the right words will come, the right actions will unfold, and understanding will deepen.

The patience cultivated between siblings is often unspoken but always felt. It's seen in the quiet support offered during tough times, the understanding that not every problem needs an immediate solution, and the acceptance that each person has their own pace and path in life. Siblings, in their own unique way, teach us that waiting is not just about enduring time but about building trust, deepening connections, and creating a foundation that withstands the test of time.

In these relationships, waiting becomes a form of love – a gentle reassurance that, no matter how much time passes, the bond remains strong. It reminds us that in every pause, there is an opportunity for growth, and in every moment of waiting, there is the potential for something beautiful to unfold.

An Example from Courtship: Patience with Ritambhara

Before Ritambhara and I got married, during the early days of our courtship, I didn't present the best version of myself. I was overwhelmed with work and entangled in challenges of a mammoth scale that demanded my full attention. I was deeply focused on resolving these issues, caught up in the immediate pressures of my career. I feared that the stress and distractions would cloud my judgement, affecting a decision that could shape my entire life.

I couldn't give Ritambhara the time or attention she deserved. I simply told her, "It will take some time." It wasn't the most reassuring response, but I needed space to navigate my challenges without the added weight of making a significant life decision.

Ritambhara, with her natural ability to listen and an even greater capacity for patience, waited. She didn't press for answers, didn't push for clarity. She understood that I was in a difficult place and gave me the time I needed. For two long months, she remained patient, waiting quietly while I sorted out my issues.

Then, after what felt like an eternity, she offered me an opportunity to explain. I remember that day vividly. We met, and she listened for hours. I poured out everything—my fears, my struggles, my worries. I explained why I had been distant and why I had asked her to wait. As I spoke, I could see her listening, really listening, with the patience of someone who genuinely wanted to understand.

Despite being an accomplished attorney with a Master's degree in law—yeah, you heard that right, a Master's in Law!—she didn't interrogate me like I was on the witness stand. No cross-examinations, no objections, no leading the witness. She just sat there, as calm as a judge on a slow day, letting me ramble on. She showed me patience, which made me think, "Wow, this woman must have been at the top of her class in patience 101!"

It was that same patience, her willingness to wait and listen without prejudice, that made all the difference. That simple yet powerful act of waiting allowed our relationship to grow and blossom into something deeper and more meaningful. It gave me the courage to open up and, ultimately, to realise that she was the one I wanted to spend my life with.

Thanks to her approach, Ritambhara is now my lovely wife. Her patience taught me a lesson that no amount of experience or knowledge could have imparted—that sometimes, the greatest gift we can give someone is the time to be heard, to be understood, and to feel safe enough to be themselves.

The Value of Waiting in Relationships: Insights from the *Bhagavad Gita*

The *Bhagavad Gita* also speaks to the idea of equanimity – of maintaining a balanced mind in all circumstances. It teaches that one should remain calm and composed, irrespective of external situations. This philosophy is incredibly relevant to our relationships. When we wait before reacting, we are practising this equanimity; we are choosing to remain steady, to not let emotions dictate our responses.

Reacting too quickly can be like throwing fuel on a fire. The flames rise higher, and before you know it, the situation has spiralled out of control. But when we wait, we allow time for the flames to subside. We give ourselves and others the space to reflect, to calm down, and to find a solution that strengthens rather than weakens our bonds.

Conclusion: The Silent Strength of Waiting

Waiting before reacting is not about suppressing emotions or denying one's feelings. It's about choosing to respond thoughtfully rather than impulsively. It's about recognising that our initial reactions are often not the most constructive. By waiting, we create space for understanding, empathy, and meaningful dialogue.

In every relationship—whether with a spouse, a friend, a parent, or a sibling—there will be moments of conflict and misunderstanding. But if we can learn to wait, to take a breath, and to listen fully before responding, we can transform these moments into opportunities for growth and deeper connection.

As I have learned from both ancient wisdom and personal experience, waiting before reacting is a powerful practice that preserves relationships, fosters trust, and ultimately brings us closer to those we care about most.

Reflection Prompts:

1. Think about a recent conflict where you reacted immediately. How did your reaction impact the situation? What might have changed if you had waited before responding?
2. Identify a relationship in your life where patience has made a positive difference. How did waiting help preserve or strengthen this relationship?

Exercise:

➤   **The 'Pause Before Responding' Challenge:** For the next seven days, practice pausing for a few seconds before responding in conversations, especially in heated or tense moments. Note how this impacts your interactions and feelings.

FAQ:

Q: How does waiting before reacting help in preserving relationships?
A: Waiting before reacting allows emotions to settle, provides time to think rationally, and prevents impulsive reactions that may damage relationships. It fosters better communication, empathy, and understanding.

'The Hot Letter' Technique

Abraham Lincoln, the 16th President of the United States, was known for his wisdom, leadership, and emotional restraint, especially during the Civil War – a time of immense pressure and conflict. One of Lincoln's strategies for preserving relationships and avoiding unnecessary conflict was his practice of writing 'hot letters'.

Whenever Lincoln felt anger or frustration towards someone, particularly his generals or political opponents, he would write a letter expressing his strong emotions. However, instead of sending the letter, he would put it aside, mark it 'never sent, never signed', and wait until he calmed down.

One famous example is his letter to General George Meade after the Battle of Gettysburg. Lincoln was deeply frustrated that Meade did not pursue the Confederate army more aggressively after the Union victory. Lincoln wrote a letter criticising Meade for missing an opportunity to end the war sooner, but he never sent it. Later, he reflected that if he had sent the letter, it could have damaged their relationship and possibly undermined the war effort.

By waiting to react, Lincoln allowed his initial emotions to settle, and he could consider the broader implications of his actions. His 'hot letter' technique shows how patience in moments of anger can prevent rash decisions, preserve important relationships, and maintain a focus on the greater good.

Closing Thoughts

Relationships are built on trust, understanding, and respect—qualities that are nurtured through patience. Waiting before reacting is not about suppressing your voice but about ensuring that what you say and do comes from a place of wisdom rather than impulse. It's in that pause, that moment of reflection, where true connection is fostered. In every conversation and every interaction, remember that the time you take to listen and think before you respond can make all the difference. Patience doesn't just preserve relationships; it strengthens them, allowing them to grow in ways that hurried reactions never could.

CHAPTER 3

Wait to Understand: Avoiding Misjudgements

In life, we often come across situations where we need to make judgements. This does not necessarily mean we are being prejudiced. The right kind of judgement is what truly sets you apart, a realisation I've come to after decades of working across domains from media to manufacturing.

Judgements define you—not your education, skills, or confidence. They shape your choices and the paths you take. A stockbroker judges price movements; call options are entirely based on timely judgements. An industry leader judges whether the business they are venturing into will succeed or fail. In my experience, judgements determine not just outcomes but the very essence of who we become.

Misjudgements, however, can ruin choices, careers, and relationships. Misjudging people or situations can lead to missed opportunities or unintended consequences. This is why it is crucial to wait before forming an opinion. Pausing allows us to gather more information, consider different perspectives, and avoid the pitfalls of a hasty decision.

Consider the story of a manager I once knew who had recently hired a new team member. The newcomer, let's call him Ajay, seemed quiet and reserved. The manager, who was used to employees who were more vocal and outgoing, quickly judged Ajay as uninterested and lacking initiative. Based on this impression, he assigned Ajay to a less challenging role, assuming he wouldn't be able to handle more responsibility.

Weeks went by, and the manager noticed that Ajay was delivering exceptional results, far exceeding the expectations for his assigned tasks. Curious, he decided to have a one-on-one conversation with Ajay. It turned out that Ajay was not only highly skilled but also incredibly innovative. He had previously worked in a high-pressure environment where speaking out of turn was frowned upon, which had made him cautious. He was keen to contribute, but he was still trying to understand the culture of the new workplace.

The manager realised that his initial judgement had been premature and unfair. If he had waited, taken the time to observe, and engaged with Ajay earlier, he could have recognised his true potential from the start. Fortunately, he was able to rectify his mistake and soon entrusted Ajay with more significant responsibilities, leading to excellent results for the team. But the manager also learned a valuable lesson: a snap judgement had almost cost him a valuable team member and a chance for growth.

This example shows how quick judgements based on surface impressions can be counterproductive. By waiting before forming an opinion, the manager could have avoided a misjudgement that nearly hindered his team's success. Waiting before judging isn't about indecision or lack of confidence; it's about clarity and wisdom. It's about trusting that, with time, the right decision will come into focus. And in that waiting, we learn that the most valuable judgements are those made with patience, understanding, and insight.

A Personal Experience: Misjudging an Employee

I recall another instance in my own company that taught me the power of waiting before judging, a lesson I'm glad I learned when I did.

One day, a manager came to me, frustrated. "We need to let him go," he insisted, referring to one of our employees who had recently started showing up late for work. "He's disrespecting our rules, setting a bad example for the team."

I could feel the heat of his frustration, but I decided to approach this differently. "Let's not rush this decision," I told him. "I'm not a fan of quick removals, especially not over a few late arrivals. Let's wait a bit and see what's going on."

Weeks passed, and the manager's patience was wearing thin. His insistence grew stronger, but I held my ground. I felt there was more to the story, something we were missing. Finally, I called the employee to my office for a talk.

When he arrived, I could see the tension in his posture and the hesitation in his eyes. "I've noticed you've been arriving late recently," I began, trying to keep my tone calm and open. "Is everything alright?"

At first, he said nothing. Just sat there, fidgeting with his hands, glancing around the room. I waited, sensing that the silence itself was a necessary pause. "Take your time," I said gently. "I'm here to understand, not to judge."

After a few moments, he finally spoke, his voice low and strained. "Sir, my wife passed away a few months ago… kidney failure," he began, his eyes welling up. "Since then, it's just been me and the kids."

He paused, and I waited again, letting him gather his thoughts. "Every morning," he continued, "I wake up my daughter and son, help them brush, bathe, get dressed… They're just seven and eleven. The elder one doesn't want me to pack her lunch because it's not how her mom used to do it, and the younger one keeps asking for his mother to help him with everything… It's a struggle every day."

As he spoke, the reality of his life unfolded before me—waking the kids, preparing meals, doing the household chores, and managing all this on his own while still trying to make it to work. The reason for his lateness became painfully clear.

At that moment, I felt a wave of humility wash over me. "I'm so sorry," I said quietly. "I can't imagine what you're going through."

He continued, "I try my best to get here on time, but sometimes... I just can't make it."

I felt a deep sense of empathy. Here was a man struggling with unimaginable grief and responsibility, and his tardiness was merely a reflection of the life he was forced to juggle. "Thank you for sharing this with me," I told him. "I appreciate your honesty, and I understand now. We'll work with you on this. Take whatever time you need."

Had I acted on the manager's recommendation and reacted hastily, we would have lost a dedicated employee and caused even more unnecessary pain. Waiting, listening, and understanding allowed us to support him in his time of need. And I'm glad I waited—sometimes, it's the only thing that truly makes a difference.

Einstein's Struggle for Acceptance

Albert Einstein, one of the most brilliant minds in history, faced significant challenges early in his career, partly due to others' misjudgements of his abilities. As a young physicist, Einstein's theories—particularly his ideas about relativity—were considered radical and were met with scepticism and resistance from many in the scientific community.

Einstein's patience was tested as he waited for years for his work to be recognised. He continued to refine his theories and write papers while working in a patent office in Bern, Switzerland. Many prominent scientists dismissed his work because it was so different from the established ideas of the time.

However, Einstein waited and persisted, confident in the validity of his ideas. He chose not to react negatively to criticism or rush to prove himself. Instead, he continued to refine his work, patiently waiting for the right time and the right evidence to support his theories.

Eventually, his patience paid off. In 1919, when astronomers observed the bending of light around the sun during a solar eclipse, Einstein's theory of general relativity was validated, catapulting him to international fame.

His experience shows that waiting to understand, rather than rushing to judgement or validation, can lead to groundbreaking discoveries and change the course of history.

Reflection Prompts:

1. Reflect on a time when you misjudged someone or a situation because you acted too quickly. How might patience have changed the outcome?
2. What are some common assumptions you make about people? How could waiting to understand help you avoid these misjudgements?

Exercise:

➤ **Patience in Listening:** Practice active listening for one week. When conversing with others, focus entirely on their words without planning your response. Note how this changes your understanding and the quality of your conversations.

FAQ:

Q: How does patience help in avoiding misjudgements?
A: Patience allows you to gather more information, observe actions over time, and understand different perspectives. This reduces the risk of making hasty conclusions based on incomplete data.

Closing Thoughts

Patience in understanding is not about being passive; it's about actively choosing to see beyond the surface. In a world that moves quickly and often judges hastily, waiting to understand is a form of wisdom and compassion. When we allow ourselves the time to look deeper, ask questions, and consider other perspectives, we open the door to more meaningful connections and richer experiences.

Remember, every person and situation is more than what meets the eye. By waiting to understand, we give ourselves the opportunity to avoid misjudgements and to see the full picture with clarity and empathy.

CHAPTER 4

Wait & Trust the Timing: When the Universe Aligns

When I look back at my life, one thing stands out above all else: the way the universe seems to have a plan of its own. I've often found myself on paths I never intended to take, only to realise much later that those very paths led me exactly where I needed to be. I believe wholeheartedly in the cosmic energy that flows through all things, that unseen force that aligns with the stars just when we think we are lost in the dark.

You already know about my decision to marry Ritambhara. If ever there was a sign of the universe aligning the stars, that was it. But I want to take you further back, beyond the boundaries of personal relationships, into a broader canvas where life itself unfolded in ways I could never have planned or predicted.

The Dream That Wasn't Meant to Be

When I first set out on my academic journey, I had a singular goal: to work for Google as a software engineer. I was preparing rigorously for my B. Tech, M. Tech, and then a PhD. Android was just emerging, and so was my ambition. I dreamed of contributing to something groundbreaking, something that brings about a change, something impactful.

But life, as it often does, had other plans. Due to an unexpected and unfortunate turn of events in my personal life, I couldn't pursue that path. I found myself at a crossroads, my dreams of Google fading into the distance. I remember feeling lost, as if the universe had thrown a curveball, shattering the vision I had so carefully constructed for myself.

I thought I had lost everything I wanted. But sometimes, when one door closes, it's because another, much larger one, is about to open.

The Universe Opens New Doors

Forced to rethink my plans, I turned my attention to a passion that had always been simmering beneath the surface: esports. I decided to create what would become one of the largest esports media platforms in the world—TalkEsport. At the time, it seemed like a shot in the dark, a diversion from the grand plans I had envisioned for myself. But I felt an undeniable pull, an energy that seemed to guide me towards this new venture.

And then, out of nowhere, came an opportunity to step into an entirely different realm: a merger and acquisition that led me to take over a chemical company—Waldies—that, at the time, was clocking in at just $5 million. Chemistry had never been my strength; in fact, it was my weakest subject in school. I found myself in a field I knew little about, running a company that made no sense to my IT-driven mind.

But the universe was weaving its intricate design, one thread at a time.

From IT Enthusiast to Chemical Conglomerate

Fast forward to today. TalkEsport, the platform I started almost on a whim, is now valued at over $5 million. Waldies, the chemical conglomerate I once stumbled upon, is on track to clock $50 million in revenues this year. I sit on the board of Waldies Ltd. as its managing director and run TalkEsport as CEO.

Was this the universe aligning the stars? Maybe. Or maybe not. Who can say what would have happened if I had stayed the course with my B. Tech, M.Tech, and PhD? Would I have made it to Google? Would I have thrived in that world? Or would I have found myself longing for something more, something different, something that fed my spirit rather than just my ambition?

What I do know is this: life brought me here, to this moment, in ways I could never have imagined. The very paths I thought were leading me away from my dreams were, in fact, guiding me toward something far greater. I found myself valued in ways I never expected, not just by my peers but by life itself. And all I had to do was wait for it to unfold.

A Poetic Justice in Waiting

There is a certain poetic justice to all of this. I was a core IT enthusiast, someone who felt at home in the world of software, algorithms, and innovation. Chemistry was my Achilles' heel, the subject that baffled and bored me. Yet, here I am, running a chemical conglomerate as the managing director with 700 people working with me, including dozens of professionals—CAs, BTechs, BScs, and even PhDs.

It's almost laughable, isn't it? The universe took a boy who struggled with chemistry and made him the leader of a chemical empire. It's as if the cosmos has a sense of humour, delighting in turning our expectations upside down. But in that twist lies a profound truth: we don't always know what's best for us. Sometimes, we just have to wait and trust that the universe does.

Trusting the Cosmic Energy

I've had countless moments in my life where I felt a force, something greater than myself, guiding my decisions. One such experience stands out. I had planned to travel to a distant city for a business meeting. Everything was set—the tickets booked, the itinerary confirmed. But on the morning of the flight, I felt a strong pull to stay back. I can't explain it; there was no logical reason behind my hesitation. It was just a feeling, a nudge from somewhere deep within. I decided to trust that feeling and cancelled my flight, even though it seemed irrational at the time.

Later that day, I found out that the very flight I was supposed to be on had encountered serious engine trouble mid-air. While the plane managed to return safely to the origin city, the incident made headlines. I remember feeling a strange mix of relief and awe. It wasn't that I believed in some miraculous intervention; rather, it was a profound reminder that, sometimes, there is a reason behind those inexplicable instincts.

This wasn't about superstition or fear—it was about trusting that inner voice, that cosmic whisper that tells you to wait, to pause, to consider. I realised that there's a deeper connection at play, a rhythm to life that we may not always understand but can learn to listen to. Sometimes, it's just about being still enough to hear that quiet voice saying, "Not yet."

Trusting the Timing of the Universe

In every culture, in every spiritual tradition, there is a belief in a force greater than ourselves. Call it God, destiny, fate, or simply the universe—it is an energy that moves through all things, aligning events and moments in ways we can't always understand. I've learned to trust that energy, to believe that there is a reason for every delay, every detour, every unexpected turn.

Waiting isn't passive; it's an act of faith. It's about trusting that the stars will align in their own time and that the universe has a way of bringing us exactly where we need to be, even if it doesn't make sense to us at the moment. It's about letting go of the need to control every outcome and surrendering to the flow of life.

The Dance of the Stars

Looking back, I see the dance of the stars, the way each one found its place in the sky, creating a constellation that was uniquely mine. I could never have drawn it myself; I could never have imagined the twists and turns that would lead me here. But I see now that every step, every stumble, every unexpected twist was part of a larger design.

Had I pushed, had I forced my way towards my original dream, I might never have discovered the joy and fulfilment I have now in my entrepreneurial journey. The universe had a better plan, a plan that required me to wait, to trust, to believe that even when things seem to fall apart, they are actually falling into place.

A Final Thought on Trusting the Timing

Observe the Universe, Don't Rush to Alter It

One of the most valuable lessons I've learned is to observe the universe without trying to rush or alter its course. There is a rhythm, a natural flow to life, and sometimes, all we need to do is pay attention. The universe sends us signals, messages, and signs if we are patient enough to notice them. These signs may not always be obvious or what we expect, but they are there, guiding us if we're willing to see them.

Instead of forcing a change or rushing to take action, try simply observing. Look around you, listen to what's happening, and notice the patterns. Often, the universe has a way of aligning things perfectly, of moving us toward where we need to be, but only if we are open to its guidance. Patience, in this context, is not a passive state but an active practice of paying attention and allowing things to unfold at their own pace.

So, the next time you feel the urge to push ahead or control every outcome, take a moment to step back. Look for the signs. Listen to that quiet, inner voice. Trust that the universe knows what it's doing. And in that waiting, you might just find that everything falls into place more perfectly than you could have ever planned.

Reflection Prompts:

1. Reflect on a moment in your life when things fell into place unexpectedly. How did waiting and trusting in the timing help?

2. How do you feel about the idea of cosmic timing or the universe aligning? Have there been instances where you felt things happened at the perfect moment?

Exercise:

➤ **Cosmic Timing Journal:** For one month, keep a journal of moments where you feel the universe has aligned things in your favour. Reflect on how waiting played a role in these experiences.

FAQ:

Q: What does it mean to trust the timing of the universe?
A: Trusting the timing means believing that things happen for a reason and at the right moment. It involves surrendering control and allowing life's natural flow to guide you.

Jobs To Apple

Steve Jobs, the co-founder of Apple Inc., is a powerful example of trusting the timing of the universe. In 1985, after a power struggle within Apple, Jobs was ousted from the company he had founded. It was a devastating blow to someone who had poured his heart and soul into building Apple from a garage startup into a major technology company.

For many years, it seemed like Jobs had lost his way. He started a new company, NeXT, which initially struggled to find its footing. However, Jobs continued to innovate and wait for the right moment. In the meantime, he acquired a small animation studio called Pixar, which, under his leadership, became a pioneer in computer animation and a wildly successful company.

In 1996, more than a decade after his departure, Apple acquired NeXT, bringing Jobs back to the company. His return was timed with the company's dire need for innovation and vision. Jobs transformed Apple's product line and launched revolutionary products like the iMac, iPod, iPhone, and iPad, leading Apple to become one of the most valuable companies in the world.

Jobs often spoke about trusting that "the dots will connect" in the future. His story illustrates that sometimes, the universe has a plan that requires us to wait. What seems like a setback can turn into a setup for something far greater than we could ever imagine.

Closing Thoughts

Life often unfolds in ways that defy our plans and expectations, and sometimes, it takes years to understand why things happened the way they did. Trusting the timing is about letting go of the need to control every aspect and allowing the universe to work its magic. It means having faith that there is a larger plan at play, even when the path seems uncertain.

As you move forward, remember that not every answer comes immediately, and not every step needs to be planned. Trust that the stars will align in their own time and that sometimes, the best we can do is wait, watch, and believe in the journey.

CHAPTER 5

The Science of Patience: Why Waiting Matters

Patience is not a virtue we often celebrate. It doesn't shout or demand attention; instead, it works quietly in the background, shaping our lives in profound ways. In a world that glorifies speed, efficiency, and instant results, patience is often seen as a burden—a painful exercise in restraint. When someone tells us to "be patient," it can feel almost like a punishment, a demand to suppress our natural instincts to act or respond.

Practically speaking, patience is painful. It's uncomfortable to wait, to hold back, to stay calm in the face of delays or frustrations. Our bodies resist it; our brains rail against it. We crave action, resolution, and quick answers. But there's another side to patience that we often overlook—a side that speaks not just to its moral or philosophical value but to its power to enhance our well-being.

Patience as Inner Strength: Standing Firm in the Storm

Patience may feel like a struggle, but it is in this struggle that our strength is built. It's not about sitting passively or doing nothing; it's about standing firm when the world seems to push us in every direction. It's a strength that grows each time we resist the impulse to react immediately, each time we choose to breathe and wait for clarity.

Neurologically, patience calms the nerves. When we resist the urge to get excited or stressed too easily, our bodies respond by maintaining a state of equilibrium. Blood pressure remains stable, and our heart rate doesn't spike. In a very real sense, patience keeps us grounded, protecting us from the physical toll of constant stress and anxiety.

Patience as a Bridge to Understanding: Nurturing Relationships with Grace

Patience is not just about waiting; it's about how we relate to others in moments of uncertainty or tension. It's the grace we extend to those around us, the understanding that we are all works in progress. Patience gives us the space to see beyond immediate frustrations and to recognise the deeper stories, the hidden struggles, and the unseen reasons behind someone's behaviour. But this isn't always easy—patience requires us to slow down, listen, and endure discomfort without jumping to conclusions or judgements.

I recall an experience with a young employee named Ravi, who had recently joined my team. Ravi was bright and enthusiastic and came up with glowing recommendations. However, as weeks went by, I noticed that he seemed to have difficulty fitting in. He was often quiet during meetings, seemed hesitant to share his ideas, and when he did speak, his thoughts seemed scattered and lacking confidence. I could sense frustration building among his teammates, who were beginning to see him as a weak link. I heard murmurs around the office suggesting that he wasn't pulling his weight.

I started to feel concerned. I had been so hopeful about Ravi's potential, and now it seemed like he might not be the right fit after all. The temptation to address the issue directly, to demand more assertiveness or a different approach, was strong. But something told me to wait—to be patient and observe a little longer. I decided not to act immediately but instead to spend some more time understanding what was going on beneath the surface.

I began to notice small things. Ravi often stayed late at the office, poring over notes and preparing for the next day. He never hesitated to ask questions but always in a quiet, almost nervous manner, as if afraid of being judged. One day, I decided to have a casual chat with him over lunch. I didn't bring up his work directly; instead, I asked about his interests, his background, and what brought him to our company.

Gradually, Ravi opened up. He shared that he came from a small town where he had rarely spoken English, and he was struggling with a language barrier that made him feel self-conscious and anxious about speaking up in meetings. He had a wealth of ideas and a deep passion for the work but felt that his lack of fluency held him back, making him hesitant to express himself fully.

This conversation changed my perspective entirely. What looked like hesitation or lack of confidence was, in fact, a fear of judgement, a feeling of inadequacy in a new environment. By choosing to wait, to understand rather than react, I discovered that the issue wasn't about competence or commitment but about creating a space where Ravi could feel comfortable and supported.

We decided to offer him some language support and encouraged a more inclusive communication style within the team. I took the time to publicly acknowledge Ravi's efforts and contributions, and my optimistic approach towards him helped build his confidence. Over time, he began to participate more actively in discussions, and soon, his unique insights became a valuable asset to our projects.

Patience had bridged the gap between misunderstanding and true understanding. It taught me that patience isn't just about giving others time – it's about giving ourselves the time to see beyond our assumptions, to ask the right questions, and to offer the right kind of support. Through patience, we build relationships that are not just professional but human, relationships that can weather any storm because they are built on a foundation of understanding and respect.

The Journey of Patience in Tandem

Patience is not just an abstract idea; it's a strategy that can shape our lives in profound ways. I've witnessed this firsthand in the journey of my younger brother-in-law, Gaurav. His story is a testament to the power of waiting with intention and trust in the timing of life.

Like me, Gaurav has always been fascinated by the concept of cosmic energy, believing that the universe has a way of aligning things at the right time. His career began humbly in Mysore, a small city in India, where he took on a challenging role at an early stage of his career. While many around him were seeking opportunities abroad, Gaurav chose to stay put, waiting for the right moment. He had his sights set on bigger horizons, particularly the United States, a place he always dreamed he would be.

While working in Mysore, he had numerous opportunities to travel to other parts of the world. But Gaurav, understanding the importance of patience, chose to stay his course. He believed that every step he took was preparing him for the bigger leap he had envisioned.

Year after year, Gaurav remained committed to his goal, strategically building his career, expanding his skills, and deepening his understanding of his industry. His patience was not passive; it was active and deliberate. He rejected several lucrative offers, knowing they would take him away from his ultimate goal. Instead, he focused on becoming indispensable in his role, gaining the experience and expertise that would make him the ideal candidate for his dream job.

And then, it happened. After years of waiting, preparing, and trusting the process, the opportunity he had been waiting for finally arrived. Gaurav was offered a position at a top consulting firm in the United States—a role that was not just another job but a realisation of his long-held dream. His patience had paid off. His wait was fruitful, proving that sometimes, strategic patience is not about waiting for what is available but about waiting for what is truly meant for you.

Gaurav's journey reminds me that patience is not just about enduring delays or setbacks. It is about recognising the value of the journey, trusting in the timing, and understanding that waiting can lead to outcomes far greater than those achieved by rushing. His story, much like mine, reflects the importance of aligning with the universe's timing and finding peace in the pauses.

Patience as a Path to Wellness: Embracing the Journey, Not Just the Destination

We often associate patience with endurance, with having to bear discomfort or delay, but there's another side to it—one that speaks to well-being and inner peace. Patience helps us find balance in our lives. It allows us to slow down, to savour the moments between moments, and to find joy in the process rather than just fixating on the end result.

In our fast-paced world, we're constantly being pushed to do more, to achieve more, to be more. But this relentless drive can be exhausting, and it often leads to burnout. I've learned that patience is a powerful antidote to this pressure. It allows us to step back, to take a deep breath, to appreciate where we are, and to find contentment in the present moment.

Neurologically, this practice of patience has profound effects. When we choose to be patient, we are choosing to stay calm and composed. Our brains release fewer stress hormones, our blood pressure remains stable, and our heartbeat stays steady. In other words, patience doesn't just feel good—it is good. It promotes mental clarity, emotional balance, and physical health.

I began to integrate mindfulness practices into my routine—not as an escape, but as a way to cultivate patience. I learned to appreciate the small moments, like the sound of rain against the window or the warmth of the sun on my face. These small acts of awareness helped me realise that life isn't a race; it's a journey to be experienced fully, with patience guiding the way.

Embracing Patience for a Healthier, Happier Life

Patience is not about suppressing our desires or remaining idle; it is an active, conscious choice to engage with life more thoughtfully. It is about finding strength in calm, nurturing our relationships with grace, and embracing the journey, no matter how long it takes.

The next time you find yourself feeling restless, remember that patience is not a punishment; it is a practice that enriches your life. It calms your mind, strengthens your heart, and creates a sense of well-being that is both deep and enduring. In waiting, we often find what we were looking for all along – a richer, fuller, more meaningful experience of life.

Reflection Prompts:

1. Consider a stressful situation where waiting made a difference. What physical or emotional changes did you notice during this time?
2. Reflect on the benefits you have experienced in life when you chose to wait. How did this impact your mental and physical well-being?

Exercise:

> **Mindful Waiting Practice:** For one week, practice mindfulness while waiting (e.g., in traffic, in line, or before a meeting). Focus on your breathing and observe your surroundings without judgement. Note how this affects your stress levels.

FAQ:

Q: How does waiting benefit our mental and physical health?
A: Waiting reduces stress, lowers blood pressure, and allows the brain to process information calmly. It encourages mindfulness and can improve overall emotional well-being.

Stanford's Marshmallow Experiment

In the late 1960s and early 1970s, psychologist Walter Mischel conducted the famous "Marshmallow Experiment" at Stanford University to study delayed gratification. Children were given a choice: they could eat one marshmallow immediately, or they could wait for 15 minutes and receive two marshmallows as a reward for their patience.

The results of this study were fascinating. Years later, researchers followed up with the children and found that those who were able to wait for the second marshmallow tended to have better life outcomes. They performed better academically, had lower levels of substance abuse, were more physically fit, and were better able to handle stress.

The experiment highlighted the science behind waiting and patience. It showed that the ability to delay gratification is a significant predictor of success in life. The findings underscore that waiting is not just a passive act; it is a vital skill that can lead to long-term rewards and achievements.

Closing Thoughts

Patience may feel like a challenge, but science shows it's one of the most powerful tools for mental, emotional, and physical well-being. It calms our nerves, improves our relationships, and helps us make better decisions. In embracing patience, we create space for clarity, creativity and growth.

So, the next time you find yourself feeling restless or pressured to act quickly, pause. Remember that waiting isn't just an act of endurance—it's an opportunity to align your actions with your values, to engage more deeply with life, and to allow your best self to emerge naturally.

Waiting Before You Take a Big Decision

In our fast-paced world, we're often pushed to make quick decisions. We're told to seize the moment, to act fast, to avoid missing out. But what if I told you that some of the best decisions are made not by rushing forward but by stepping back and waiting? What if, instead of making snap decisions, we allowed ourselves the time to let our thoughts settle, to sleep on ideas, and to let the subconscious mind work its quiet magic?

I've learned that waiting before making a big decision can be one of the most powerful tools at our disposal. It's not about procrastination or indecision; it's about giving our minds the space to explore possibilities we might not immediately see.

The Power of the Subconscious Mind: Letting Ideas Marinate

There's a reason why we often hear the phrase, "Let me sleep on it." Our brains don't stop working when we go to bed; in fact, the subconscious mind is at its most active during sleep. It's when we're not consciously thinking that some of the most innovative and thought-provoking ideas emerge. Studies have shown that sleep can help consolidate memories, solve problems, and even spark creativity.

I've seen this play out in my own life many times. For instance, when I had to decide on a brand name, I spent hours—days, even—searching for the perfect choice. I tried everything from brainstorming to consulting with colleagues, but nothing seemed to fit. The mistake I made was trying to force a decision before the end of each day, believing that I had to resolve it quickly. What I realised, eventually, was that I needed to let my mind rest and sleep on the decision.

When I finally did, something remarkable happened. One morning, I woke up with a name in mind that felt right. It wasn't something I had consciously thought of the day before, but it emerged in the quiet space of my subconscious. That's when I understood the value of waiting, of allowing my mind the freedom to explore possibilities without pressure.

The Magic of Sleep: Where Decisions Take Shape

Science supports this idea as well. When we sleep, our brains process information differently. Sleep is not just a break for our conscious minds; it's an active process where the brain organises, consolidates, and integrates experiences from the day. This is why some of our best ideas or solutions come to us after a good night's rest.

I've applied this principle beyond just naming a brand. Whenever I'm faced with a significant decision—whether it's a business strategy, a partnership, or a creative project—I make it a point to pause, to wait, and to sleep on it. I've found that waiting allows me to see things from new angles, to connect dots that weren't visible before, and to make choices with greater clarity and confidence.

For instance, when I am drafting important emails or journal articles, I never rush to hit send or publish. I save my drafts, let them sit for a day or two, and revisit them with fresh eyes. Often, I find myself making subtle but important changes—removing a phrase that felt too harsh or adding a point that strengthens the message. These small adjustments can make a big difference, and they come from waiting, from giving myself time to reflect and refine.

The Cool-Off Period: A Deliberate Pause for Clarity

One strategy I've come to rely on over the years is the concept of the **cool-off period**—a deliberate pause before making any significant decision. Whether I am considering launching a new brand, buying a property, divesting shares, or entering into a partnership, I always prefer a candid delay. This pause doesn't need to have a strict agenda; it's simply a period where I step back, breathe, and let things settle.

The length of this cool-off period is subjective and varies for each individual. For some, it might be a day; for others, it could be weeks or even months. The key is to allow enough time for emotions to cool, for facts to surface, and for intuition to guide. In my experience, this cool-off period has often revealed crucial details or insights that I might have overlooked in the heat of the moment.

There have been many instances where, during this period of reflection, I've discovered a piece of information, a potential risk, or a hidden opportunity that fundamentally changed my decision. The beauty of the cool-off period is that it allows space for both conscious analysis and subconscious reflection. It's a time to let the dust settle, to observe without pressure, and to give our minds a chance to piece together the full picture.

I've come to see this period not as hesitation or avoidance but as a strategic pause – a moment to gather all the fragments of thought and intuition into a cohesive understanding. It's a simple yet profound practice that has saved me from hasty choices and led to more thoughtful, aligned decisions.

Finding Your Own Time Frame: Personalising the Wait

One of the most valuable lessons I've learned is that there isn't a one-size-fits-all approach to waiting. The length of time you wait before making a decision can vary depending on the situation, your intuition, and your personal process. For some decisions, a few hours might suffice; for others, it could take days or even weeks.

When I'm working on a significant project or making a crucial decision, I've come to trust my own sense of timing. I wait until I feel a sense of calm, quiet confidence that the decision is right. That's when I know I'm ready to act. This waiting period isn't about hesitation; it's about allowing ideas to mature, emotions to settle, and insights to surface.

Embracing the Wait: Trusting the Process

Waiting before taking a big step is about trusting the process, trusting that in the quiet moments, our minds are still working, still creating, and still solving problems. It's about understanding that clarity often comes not from forcing an answer but from allowing it to emerge naturally.

So, the next time you're faced with a significant decision, resist the urge to rush. Instead, give yourself the gift of time. Sleep on it, sit with it, and let your subconscious mind do its work. You might be surprised by the insights that come to you, the innovative solutions that appear, and the peace you find in waiting.

Because sometimes, the best decisions are those we allow ourselves to wait for.

Reflection Prompts:

1. Think about a significant decision you're currently facing or recently made. Did you give yourself enough time to consider all the possibilities? What would have happened if you had waited a bit longer?

2. Recall a time when waiting before making a big decision led to a better outcome. What insights did you gain during the waiting period that influenced your decision?

Exercises:

➤ **The 24-Hour Rule:** For the next few big decisions, commit to waiting at least 24 hours before making the final call. Record any changes in your perspective, thoughts, or feelings during that time.

➤ **Mind Mapping:** Take a big decision you're contemplating and create a mind map. Write down all the factors, pros and cons, and potential outcomes. Let this map sit for a day, then revisit it to see if new ideas or options emerge.

FAQ:

Q: How does waiting help when making big decisions?
A: Waiting before making a big decision allows time for your subconscious to process information, reduces emotional impulsiveness, and often provides greater clarity. It enables you to weigh all options, consider different perspectives, and ultimately make a more thoughtful and aligned choice.

The Inception of Harry Potter

J.K. Rowling, the author of the globally successful "Harry Potter" series, embodies the power of waiting before taking a big step. After conceiving the idea for the story in 1990, Rowling spent years developing the characters and the magical world of Hogwarts. She wrote the manuscript for the first book, "Harry Potter and the Philosopher's Stone," while dealing with numerous personal challenges, including the death of her mother, a divorce, and raising her daughter as a single mother on welfare.

Rowling faced multiple rejections when she started sending her manuscript to publishers. Over the course of a year, twelve publishers turned it down. Many authors might have rushed to self-publish or abandoned the idea altogether. Instead, Rowling waited patiently for the right opportunity. She continued refining her manuscript and stayed resilient in her belief in her story.

Finally, a small publisher, Bloomsbury, accepted her book for publication after the CEO's eight-year-old daughter loved the first chapter and insisted on reading more. Even then, Rowling was advised to get a day job, as "there was little money in children's books." Yet, she trusted the timing and continued working on the subsequent books without rushing their release.

Rowling's patience paid off. "Harry Potter" went on to become one of the most beloved book series of all time, with millions of copies sold worldwide. Her story shows that sometimes, waiting and trusting the process—rather than rushing decisions or compromising—can lead to unimaginable success.

Conclusion: The Quiet Power of Waiting

In a world that demands urgency, choosing to wait can feel counterintuitive, even uncomfortable. Yet, the act of waiting before making a big decision is not a sign of indecision or hesitation; it's a profound exercise in wisdom and trust. It's about understanding that the answers we seek often reside beyond our immediate reach, urging us to pause, reflect, and give space for deeper thoughts and intuition to surface.

Waiting isn't a passive state; it's a deliberate act of engagement with ourselves and the world around us. It's about giving our subconscious mind the space to work its magic, about letting ideas marinate and mature, about embracing the natural rhythm of decision-making without forcing a premature outcome. By stepping back and observing rather than rushing ahead, we allow clarity to emerge in its own time.

So, when faced with your next big decision, resist the urge to rush. Instead, give yourself the gift of time – the time to reflect, to let thoughts simmer, and to let the subconscious mind explore possibilities that may not be immediately visible. Trust that in waiting, you are giving yourself the best chance to make a decision that is not only well-informed but also deeply aligned with who you are and what truly matters.

Remember, the universe often has a way of revealing the right path at the right moment. In the quiet of waiting, we find our truest wisdom.

CHAPTER 7

Waiting Through Uncertainty: Embracing the Unknown

Reflecting on my life's journey, I see a pattern: a series of crossroads, each filled with uncertainty. I've found myself repeatedly standing at these intersections, unsure of what lies ahead. When I look back, I realise that every time I waited through these moments—without rushing into decisions, without forcing an outcome—I ended up exactly where I needed to be. I am where I am today, not because I always knew what to do but because I trusted in the power of waiting.

This wasn't easy. Uncertainty is uncomfortable; it challenges our very instinct for control. We crave clarity, a clear path, a guarantee that things will work out as we hope. But life rarely offers such assurances. I've come to understand that there's a hidden strength in waiting through uncertainty – a strength that comes from embracing the unknown, from trusting that the universe, or perhaps a higher power, has a plan beyond what we can immediately see.

Linking Back to the Journey: The Moments That Defined My Path

When I decided to abandon my pursuit of a career at Google, it felt like stepping into a void. I had spent years preparing for this path, dreaming of what it could mean, only to have those plans upended by unforeseen circumstances. But instead of scrambling to find a new direction immediately, I chose to wait. I let the uncertainty linger, trusting that a new path would reveal itself in time.

During that period of waiting, TalkEsport came into existence—not as a deliberate choice but as an organic evolution of my passions and experiences. Had I rushed into another tech role or jumped at the first opportunity, I might have missed the chance to create something that aligned with my deeper purpose. The universe, it seems, had a different plan for me, and it unfolded precisely when I allowed myself to wait in the face of uncertainty.

The Strength Found in the Unknown

The lesson I learned is that waiting through uncertainty is not about inaction; it's about holding space for possibilities that we cannot yet see. It's about having the patience to sit with discomfort, to let the fog clear naturally, rather than trying to force clarity. Each time I have waited through the unknown, I have found that life has a way of aligning itself in unexpected and remarkable ways.

When the opportunity to acquire Waldies, a chemical company, presented itself, it felt completely out of sync with my background in media and technology. I could have dismissed it as a distraction or a deviation from my path. But instead, I chose to wait. I chose to let the idea settle, to explore it without immediate judgement, and to trust that if it was meant to be, it would become clear in time.

And it did. Over weeks and months, as I waited, I saw the potential for growth, for new challenges, and for learning that went beyond the obvious. Waiting allowed me to see this opportunity not as a random detour but as a meaningful step forward.

Navigating the Unknown at My Company: Trusting the Process

I could never have anticipated the challenges I would face with my new role at Waldies Ltd. When I was first approached with the opportunity, I didn't even know whether to join the company or not. I stepped into the role of Vice President of Business Development with complete faith in the Almighty, who had put me in this situation in the first place.

The environment was uncertain and unfamiliar, and I had to navigate new waters without a clear map. The only thing that remained under my control was waiting—waiting for the right moment to make strategic moves, to build relationships, and to set the course for growth. This wasn't about infinite waiting; it was about waiting with intention, with a purpose, with patience.

From $5 million in revenues to $50 million in less than five years and progressing my way to become the youngest managing director amidst a global pandemic, potential world conflicts, and substantial changes in global economic conditions, we were able to sail through. The anchor that held us steady in those tumultuous times was the patience I chose to possess. Waiting through uncertainty, not in fear, but in faith, allowed us to weather the storms and emerge stronger than before.

Embracing the Unknown: Trusting What We Cannot See

What I've realised is that uncertainty is not something to fear; it is something to embrace. It is in the unknown that we often find the most profound opportunities for growth. We are conditioned to believe that we must always have a plan, always know our next steps, and always be in control. But real growth happens when we surrender to the unknown and trust that even in the midst of uncertainty, there is a plan unfolding.

I have come to see uncertainty as a kind of invitation – an invitation to be open, to be curious, to explore what life has to offer without the need for immediate answers. It's an invitation to pause, to wait, and to let things unfold as they are meant to.

The Wisdom in Waiting: Allowing Life to Guide Us

Waiting is not a passive act; it is an act of profound wisdom. It's about recognising that we don't have all the answers and that sometimes the best thing we can do is to step back and let life guide us. When we wait, we give ourselves the space to listen to our inner voice, to notice the subtle signs around us, and to make decisions not out of fear or haste, but out of clarity and purpose.

In every period of uncertainty I've faced, I've learned to ask myself, "What if I just waited a little longer? What might I see that I couldn't see before?" Often, it is in that waiting that the most unexpected and beautiful outcomes emerge.

Final Thoughts: Finding Peace in the Pause

So, when life feels uncertain, when you don't know which way to turn, remember this: Sometimes, the best thing you can do is nothing at all. Wait. Trust that the answers will come when the time is right, and in the meantime, the universe is working in ways you cannot yet see. Embrace the unknown, not with fear, but with curiosity and patience.

Because it is often in the waiting stage that life reveals its most precious gifts.

Reflection Prompts:

1. Think about a time when you faced uncertainty in your life. How did you respond? What did waiting through that period teach you about yourself or the situation?
2. Consider how you typically handle uncertainty. Do you rush to resolve it, or can you stay with it, trusting that clarity will come in time?

Exercises:

➤ **Mindful Embracing of Uncertainty:** Practice sitting with uncertainty in small, everyday situations. For instance, when waiting for an answer or a result, notice any discomfort that arises. Breathe through it, acknowledging that it's okay not to have all the answers right away.

➤ **Uncertainty Journal:** Keep a journal for a month, documenting situations where you felt uncertain. Reflect on how you felt, what you did, and what the outcome was. How did patience play a role?

FAQ:

Q: How can I become more comfortable with uncertainty?
Becoming comfortable with uncertainty involves recognising that it's a natural part of life. Focus on staying grounded in the present, directing your energy toward what you can influence, and releasing the need to control everything else. It helps to remember that uncertainty often brings opportunities and growth that wouldn't arise otherwise.

Anecdote: The Apollo 13 Mission

In April 1970, NASA's Apollo 13 mission, intended to be the third crewed mission to land on the moon, faced a life-threatening crisis. Just two days into the mission, an oxygen tank exploded on board, crippling the spacecraft and leaving the three astronauts—Jim Lovell, Jack Swigert, and Fred Haise— stranded 200,000 miles from Earth. With limited power, dwindling supplies, and an uncertain path back to Earth, the crew and mission control were thrust into a state of extreme uncertainty.

The world watched anxiously as NASA's flight director, Gene Kranz, and his team at mission control worked tirelessly to bring the crew home safely. Throughout the ordeal, Kranz and his team exhibited extraordinary patience and calm. Instead of rushing to decisions in panic, they methodically analysed every piece of data, calculated the remaining fuel and power, and created new procedures on the fly.

Kranz famously declared, "Failure is not an option," but his team knew that success would require waiting through the uncertainty—trusting their training, knowledge, and instinct. The astronauts, too, had to embrace the unknown, waiting for long periods with no idea if their improvised solutions would work.

After nearly 90 hours of waiting and uncertainty, the crew safely splashed down in the Pacific Ocean. The successful return of Apollo 13 became known as NASA's "successful failure," demonstrating that patience, careful planning, and faith in the face of the unknown can turn potential disasters into incredible triumphs.

Closing Thoughts

Uncertainty is a natural part of life, and waiting through it is often the most challenging thing to do. But it is in these moments of not knowing that we find our true strength. Waiting through uncertainty teaches us to trust ourselves, to rely on our inner resilience, and to find peace amidst the unknown. It's not about having all the answers; it's about being open to the journey, embracing each twist and turn with curiosity and courage.

So, when you find yourself standing at a crossroads, unsure of what comes next, remember that it's okay not to have all the answers. Trust the process, wait with purpose, and let life guide you where you are meant to be.

CHAPTER 8

Purposeful Pause: Turning Wait into Growth

But what if we shifted that perspective? What if waiting, rather than being an empty pause, was a purposeful space filled with potential for growth, learning, and self-discovery? In my journey, I've found that the moments when life seemed to stand still were actually the most powerful catalysts for change. They were the moments that shaped who I am today.

Waiting with intention is not about doing nothing. It's about engaging with the present moment, using the pause to prepare, reflect, and evolve. It's about making the most of the in-between spaces in our lives—the ones that often go unnoticed but hold the greatest opportunities for growth.

Waiting with Intention: Finding Meaning in the Pause

There were many times when I felt like I was waiting for something to happen—waiting for a business opportunity to come through, for a decision to be made, for the right time to take a big step. But rather than seeing this waiting period as dead time, I began to understand that it was a chance to engage actively with life.

When TalkEsport was still in its infancy, there were long periods where progress seemed slow, and results were not immediately visible. I could have let frustration take over or tried to force things to happen, but instead, I chose to wait actively. I used this time to deepen my understanding of the industry, build a network, and refine our strategies. These actions, taken during the waiting periods, laid the groundwork for our future successes. Waiting became a time of preparation, not procrastination.

Turning Waiting into Action: The Art of Active Engagement

Active waiting is not a passive act; it's a deliberate choice to make the most of the waiting period by engaging in meaningful activities that move us forward, even if progress isn't immediately visible. I've found that these periods are opportunities to sharpen my skills, deepen my relationships, and realign my goals with my core values.

During these pauses, I often immerse myself in learning. Whether it's diving into new market trends, acquiring a skill I've long wanted to develop, or exploring unfamiliar territories in my field, these moments of focused learning have consistently paid off in unexpected ways. The knowledge gained during these times has often provided me with the edge I needed when opportunities finally arose.

Building relationships is another critical aspect of active waiting. In business, patience often requires giving others the time they need to align with your vision. Instead of pushing forward alone, I've used these waiting periods to strengthen my connections with colleagues, partners, and mentors. These relationships, nurtured during times of patience, have often led to new opportunities, collaborations, and insights that might not have emerged otherwise.

A Tale of Two Friends: Patience and Strategic Growth in the Corporate World

I have two friends, both of whom I've had the privilege of knowing for many years. I've seen them grow, evolve, and navigate the complexities of their careers with remarkable determination. They each work for top consulting firms with global reach, and in the last few years, both have faced significant challenges in their respective sectors. As markets dipped and economic conditions became increasingly uncertain, a wave of resignations swept through their companies. Many sought opportunities elsewhere, hoping for greater stability or faster growth. My friends, too, found themselves standing at a crossroads, questioning whether they should move on or stay put.

We had countless conversations during this period. I remember sitting with them, weighing the options, examining the gaps that were beginning to appear as more and more people left. Both friends were ambitious and driven, eager to make their mark, but they were also thoughtful and reflective. We discussed the value of staying versus the risks of leaving and the potential for growth that lay hidden within the chaos.

Together, we explored a different perspective: what if they didn't rush to find something new? What if, instead, they chose to wait—strategically, intentionally—and use this period of uncertainty to their advantage? We talked about the power of waiting, not passively, but with purpose.

They decided to stay. But staying didn't mean standing still. It meant embracing the gaps created by others' departures, taking on new roles, and expanding their knowledge beyond their initial scope. They immersed themselves in different departments, offered support wherever it was needed, and upskilled in areas they had previously overlooked. They made themselves invaluable by being present, reliable, and ready to take on new challenges.

This decision to wait and work purposefully during uncertain times transformed their careers. Today, both of them are CFOs of two of the most important regions for their respective companies. They have become leaders, not because they rushed to the next opportunity but because they waited, watched, and acted when the time was right.

Their stories are a testament to the power of waiting with intention. In a world that often glorifies speed and urgency, they choose to pause, to prepare, and to engage actively with the moment. And in doing so, they found not just career success but a deeper understanding of their own strengths and the unique value they bring to their companies.

Finding Fulfilment in the Process: Redefining Success

We are often conditioned to measure success by visible achievements—the deals closed, the goals reached, the milestones passed. But waiting teaches us that success is not just about the destination; it's about the journey. The moments when we seem to be standing still are often the most critical for our growth.

I've learned to find fulfilment not just in reaching a goal but in the steps I take toward it, however slow they might seem. Waiting with purpose has taught me to enjoy the process, to find satisfaction in the small, daily progress, and to trust that every moment of waiting is a step forward, even if it doesn't feel like it.

Closing the Loop: The Continuation of the Journey

Waiting is not a detour; it is part of the path. By engaging with the pause actively, we turn waiting into a purposeful, meaningful part of our journey. It's not about standing still; it's about preparing for what comes next with clarity, intention, and readiness that only comes from fully embracing the wait.

Reflection Prompts:

1. Reflect on a time when waiting allowed you to grow or develop a skill you hadn't initially considered. What did you learn from that period of waiting?

2.   Think about areas in your life where you could introduce a purposeful pause. What might you gain from waiting instead of rushing?

Exercises:

➤ **Skill Development Pause:** Identify a skill or hobby you have been putting off. Instead of diving in immediately, create a structured plan for how you will use any waiting periods to gradually build this skill.

➤ **Weekly Reflection Time:** Set aside 30 minutes at the end of each week to reflect on moments where you chose to wait and how they contributed to your growth. Note down any insights or lessons.

FAQ:

Q: How can waiting contribute to personal growth?
A: Waiting gives you time to think, reflect, and gain a deeper understanding of yourself and your goals. It can lead to new insights, skill development, and a more deliberate and thoughtful approach to life's challenges and opportunities.

Michelangelo & Sistine Chapel

Michelangelo, one of the greatest artists of all time, was initially reluctant to take on the commission to paint the ceiling of the Sistine Chapel. He considered himself a sculptor, not a painter and was already engaged in sculpting the tomb of Pope Julius II. When asked to paint the chapel's ceiling, he tried to avoid the project, feeling that it was outside his expertise.

However, after much persuasion and contemplation, Michelangelo agreed. But he did not rush into it. He spent months studying the architecture of the chapel, preparing sketches, and envisioning how the frescoes could convey biblical stories in a way that had never been seen before. He took time to master the art of fresco painting, a medium with which he was not familiar.

Michelangelo's patience and willingness to pause before diving into the work allowed him to grow as an artist. Instead of rushing the project to prove himself, he took the time to experiment, learn, and refine his techniques. He spent four years working on the chapel, lying on his back on scaffolding, painstakingly painting over 5,000 square feet of frescoes.

The result was a masterpiece that changed the course of Western art forever. Michelangelo's "Creation of Adam" and other scenes on the Sistine

Chapel ceiling are considered some of the greatest achievements in art history. This anecdote illustrates that waiting and taking a purposeful pause can lead to immense personal growth and creative breakthroughs.

Closing Thoughts

Waiting is often seen as wasted time, but it doesn't have to be. By choosing to wait with intention, you transform pauses into opportunities for growth, learning, and self-discovery. These moments, when embraced, become fertile ground for reflection, creativity, and preparation. Instead of seeing waiting as a delay, view it as a valuable space that allows you to become stronger, wiser, and more aligned with your purpose.

In these pauses, you find the chance to engage with life more deeply, explore new possibilities, and grow in ways you never imagined.

CHAPTER 9

Waiting For Seasons – The Sync of the Nature

In our quest for control, we often try to figure everything out at once. We want the answers, the results, the success—immediately, if possible. Yet, life doesn't work that way. Much like nature, life has its own rhythm, its own seasons, and its own pace. The sun rises and sets on its schedule; the moon waxes and wanes in its own time. Crops don't grow faster just because we wish them to—they follow their own natural cycle, and no amount of impatience can speed up their growth.

I've come to realise that trying to force things to happen before their time is as futile as trying to make mangoes ripen in the winter. The universe moves according to its own timeline, and there is profound wisdom in learning to trust that timing.

The Rhythm of Life: Learning from Nature's Cycles

If you observe the natural world, you'll notice that everything happens in its own time. The seasons change, the tides rise and fall, and plants grow, bloom, and wither—all in a rhythm that has existed for millennia. There's no rush, no urgency—only a quiet, steady progression. Nature is patient. It doesn't hurry, yet everything is accomplished in its due course.

When I look at my own life, I see the same patterns mirrored. There were periods when I wanted things to happen quickly—whether it was launching a new product, expanding into a new market, or making a major life decision. But each time I tried to force the pace, I found myself facing resistance. It was only when I learned to align myself with the natural flow of events rather than pushing against it that I discovered a sense of peace and clarity.

Consider the process of farming. A farmer knows that planting a seed is only the beginning. There is a natural cycle that must be respected – a time to nurture the soil, to water the plants, to wait for the sun and rain to do their work. The harvest will come, but only when the time is right. There is no rushing it, no shortcutting the process. The farmer waits, trusting in the natural order of things, knowing that the fruits will come when they are ready.

Embracing Patience: The Wisdom in Not Knowing

In our society, there is constant pressure to have everything figured out, to know exactly what we're doing, where we're going, and how we're going to get there. But life is not a linear path; it's a series of cycles, twists, and turns that often defy our expectations. And that's okay. In fact, it's more than okay—it's necessary for growth.

There is a profound freedom in allowing yourself to not have all the answers. When I first considered acquiring Waldies, the chemical company, I was far outside my comfort zone. The decision didn't come quickly, and there was a lot I didn't know. But I waited. I took my time to explore the unknowns, to ask questions, and to let the answers come in their own time. This patience allowed me to see the opportunity for what it truly was—a chance to grow, to learn, and to challenge myself in new ways.

Finding Peace in the Natural Order: Letting Life Unfold

Waiting for the right season isn't always easy, especially when we're eager for change, progress, or results. But I've found that trusting the natural order of things brings a deeper peace – a sense of calm that comes from knowing that everything has its time and place.

When I faced difficult decisions or uncertain periods in my career, I often felt the temptation to rush ahead, to find a solution quickly, to resolve the tension immediately. But I learned to wait, to allow things to unfold in their own time, and to trust that life has a rhythm that I cannot always understand but must respect.

Just as the farmer waits for the harvest, trusting that the seeds he planted will eventually bear fruit, we too must learn to trust that our efforts, our dreams, and our desires will manifest when the time is right. Sometimes, the most powerful action we can take is to step back, to let go, and to allow life to unfold naturally, without trying to force or control the outcome.

Letting Go of the Urge to Control: Trusting in the Process

There is a natural tendency to want to control every aspect of our lives, to have everything planned out perfectly. But in doing so, we often overlook the beauty of the unknown, the surprises that life has in store, and the lessons that come from waiting.

I've learned to let go of this urge to control, to embrace the uncertainty, and to trust that there is a time for everything – a time to plant and a time to reap, a time to push forward and a time to step back, a time to act and a time to wait.

In the end, by aligning ourselves with the natural rhythms of life, we find that we don't need to rush, to force, or to know everything all at once. We can find peace in the waiting, knowing that just like the seasons, everything will unfold in its own time.

So, the next time you feel the urge to rush, to figure it all out, or to have all the answers immediately, remember that life has its own rhythm. Trust that there is a season for everything and that in the waiting, there is wisdom, growth, and beauty.

Ultimately, patience is not something you master overnight – it's something you practice daily, in every moment of waiting. As you navigate your path, remember to trust the process, to honour the natural rhythms of life, and to find peace in the pauses. Because often, it is in the waiting that we discover who we are meant to be.

Reflection Prompts:

1. Reflect on a time when you tried to rush something in your life, only to realise that the natural timing was beyond your control. How did that experience change your perspective?
2. Think about a season or cycle in your life that required patience. What did you learn from waiting for the right timing?

Exercises:

- ➤ **Nature Walk Reflection:** Spend time in nature observing the natural cycles—like the blooming of flowers or the setting of the sun. Reflect on how these natural rhythms can teach us about waiting and trusting the timing of life.
- ➤ **Seasonal Planning:** Align a personal goal with a natural season. For instance, use spring as a time for planting new ideas, summer for growth, autumn for harvesting insights, and winter for reflection. Note how aligning with these cycles feels.

FAQ:

Q: What does it mean to wait for the right season, and how does it apply to life?

A: Waiting for the right season means understanding that everything has its time and place. Just as crops grow best in their specific seasons, our plans and actions often flourish when aligned with the natural flow and rhythm of life. Rushing against this rhythm can lead to unnecessary struggle and missed opportunities.

The Patience of a Farmer

Masanobu Fukuoka, a Japanese farmer and philosopher, is renowned for developing the concept of "natural farming," a method that aligns agricultural practices with the natural cycles and rhythms of the environment. In his book, "The One-Straw Revolution," Fukuoka describes how he abandoned conventional farming techniques, which relied heavily on chemicals, pesticides, and over-cultivation, in favour of a more patient, harmonious approach to farming.

Fukuoka's method, often called "do-nothing farming," was based on observing and understanding the natural processes of plants, animals, and soil. He believed that by waiting and allowing nature to take its course, farmers could achieve better results than through forced intervention. For example, rather than ploughing the fields, he allowed weeds and cover crops to grow, which naturally improved soil fertility and prevented erosion.

His approach required extraordinary patience, as it took years for his farm to yield results comparable to conventional methods. However, Fukuoka's patience paid off. Over time, his fields became more fertile, his crops healthier, and his yields comparable to those of modern farms—without using synthetic chemicals or intensive labour.

Fukuoka's story illustrates that nature operates on its own schedule, and by syncing with these natural rhythms, rather than trying to control them, we can achieve harmony and sustainability. His philosophy teaches us to trust the natural process and understand that everything happens in its own season, reinforcing the value of waiting and observing rather than forcing outcomes.

Closing Thoughts

Just like the cycles of nature, our lives move through seasons. There are times of growth and times of rest, times of clarity and times of confusion. The key is to honour each season, to trust the natural rhythms of life, and to find peace in knowing that everything unfolds in its own time. Don't rush the process or try to force outcomes; instead, embrace the pauses, the waiting, and the seasons of uncertainty.

Trust that just as the Earth knows when to bloom and when to rest, so too does your life know when it is time to move forward and when it is time to wait. Find comfort in the rhythm and let it guide you towards your next season of growth.

As we conclude our journey through the chapters of patience, remember that life, much like nature, has its seasons. There's a time to plant, a time to grow, a time to harvest, and a time to rest. Trust in the process, allow life to unfold in its own time and find peace in the waiting.

For in those quiet pauses, we often discover the most profound truths about ourselves and the world around us.

Conclusion

As I arrive at the conclusion of this journey—both in writing this book and living the experiences that inspired it—I am reminded once more of the quiet power of patience. Patience is not simply a matter of letting time pass; it is about learning to live fully in the spaces between moments, embracing uncertainties, and trusting that everything will unfold in its own perfect time.

Throughout these pages, I have shared the lessons I've gathered from waiting—whether it was waiting to truly understand others, waiting for the right opportunities to present themselves, or simply waiting for life to reveal its next steps. In each pause, I found purpose; in each moment of stillness, I discovered growth.

Patience has taught me to trust in the greater timing of the universe, to recognise that there are forces at work far beyond my understanding, and to believe that things happen precisely when they are meant to. It has shown me that our rush to control outcomes often blinds us to the gifts that only come when we allow life to follow its natural rhythm.

I hope this book has offered you a different perspective on patience—one that is not about passivity or inaction but about engaging with life more mindfully. Patience is a choice we make every day, in every interaction, and in every decision. It is a practice, a discipline, and ultimately, a path to deeper understanding and fulfilment.

Remember, this book is not a definitive guide or a manual on how to live with patience. It is a reflection of my journey, my observations, and my learnings. I have aimed to make it as practical and relatable as possible, hoping that somewhere within these pages, you find something that resonates, challenges, or even inspires you to embrace your own moments of waiting.

Life is not a race, and there is no finish line. It is a beautiful, unpredictable journey that unfolds in its own way, in its own time. So, as you move forward, I encourage you to find peace in the pauses, to trust in the natural rhythms of life, and to wait with purpose—knowing that each moment holds its own meaning and each season brings its own gifts.

Thank you for walking this path with me. May your waiting bring you wisdom, and may your patience guide you to places beyond your wildest dreams.

What if Waiting Feels Uncertain?

If you've made it this far into the book, you've likely given a lot of thought to the concept of patience and waiting. But I want to acknowledge something important: waiting isn't always easy, and sometimes it doesn't lead to the outcomes we hope for. You may find yourself questioning the process, wondering if you're waiting for something that may never come, or feeling disheartened when the results don't align with your expectations.

I want to remind you that patience is not a guarantee; it's a practice, a mindset, and a way of engaging with life that prioritises growth, understanding, and perspective over immediate results. There will be times when waiting doesn't seem to pay off, when the answers remain elusive, and when the path forward is still unclear.

And that's okay.

Life is complex, and not everything follows a predictable pattern. The outcomes of our waiting are influenced by countless factors—some within our control and many beyond it. The true value of patience lies not just in what it brings but in how it shapes us as individuals. It teaches us resilience, humility, and the ability to find peace even if things don't take place as planned.

If you're feeling uncertain or disappointed, know that these feelings are part of the journey. Patience is not about perfection; it's about perseverance. It's about learning to navigate the ups and downs of life with grace, understanding that even when things don't turn out as we hoped, there is still value in the process.

So, if you've tried waiting and the results haven't been what you expected, I encourage you not to lose heart. Reflect on what you've learned, consider how you've grown, and remember that life's greatest lessons often come from the moments when things don't go as planned.

In the end, patience is not just about the outcomes; it's about how we respond to the challenges along the way. And sometimes, the most important thing we can do is simply keep going, keep waiting, and keep believing that, in time, things will align as they are meant to—even if we don't yet know how or when.

Acknowledgements

I want to thank my Maa and my grandmother, who I truly believe possess a natural positive energy that lights up our lives. With her around, it always feels like things just fall into place, as if her presence makes everything easier.

To my father, Shri Sushil Ojha, I owe so much for your endless pieces of advice that guide me each day. And to my mother, whose love, care, and unwavering support have been my anchor through every high and low, I am forever grateful.

To my two wonderful sisters – Sangita and Kavita, who have played a vital role in making me who I am today.

To my wife, thank you for simply being you. Your patience, strength, and grace inspire me in ways I can't even put into words.

To my friends, thank you for always cheering me on and pushing me to follow my passions. A special shout-out to Sharad Jain for being there through thick and thin and for teaching me so much about patience and the art of truly listening.

To my incredible colleagues, thank you for showing up every day with resilience and heart. You make every challenge worth facing and every success so much sweeter.

And finally, to my dear Khushi and Garvit—love, and only love.

––––